MW00934657

**Discipleship Essentials: Prayer**

# Welcome to the Proverbs 31 Business Woman Community!

**It's an honor to serve you!**

Be sure to connect with Angelica on all of her social media pages. You can follow her for daily inspiration, encouragement, resources to grow in your walk with Christ as a woman, wife, mother, friend, and leader. She is committed to making disciples and equipping you along the way! Join us!

Facebook
Twitter
Instagram
Pinterest
Snapchat

@angelicakduncan

*You can register for this Bible Study and find all of the materials and resources I recommend for you to use for this study! Grab them here:*

*https://proverbs31businesswoman.com/prayer-bible-study*
**Let's get started!**

**Dance with the King!**

*Angelica*

# Table of Contents

# Preface

I was 12 or 13 years old, when my church offered "The School of Prayer." Even though it was designed by adults and for adults, two children signed up for the school. I was one of them. In that school, I learned everything about prayer, praise, worship, intercession, and so much more! I even received the gift of speaking in tongues!

Let me tell you, The School of Prayer had a huge impact on my life! I graduated fully equipped as a 13 year old to pray fervently, earnestly, and wholeheartedly. I could confidently petition the heart of God about matters and know that he would not only hear my prayers, but he would answer them.

**You see, being a Christian is one thing. Being a Disciple of Christ is another.** Prayer is a biblical discipline that Jesus taught the disciples. In this day and time, it seems many have forsaken basic biblical truths and Christian discipline. We've exchanged them for all kinds of distractions, dangling carrots on a string, and empty promises of prosperity. More now that ever, the Body of Christ is inundated with attacks, by the enemy, from marriages, children, jobs, finances, health...you name it! Sadly many do not know how to effectively fight against satan and walk in victory here on earth. We are wasting time fighting one another, complaining about circumstances, and not doing much to pierce the darkness and reveal God's Glory in the earth.

Ask yourself this question (and answer it honestly):

*If someone were to ask you to prayer for a very serious situation, in their lives, do you have the confidence and boldness to petition God, know that He hears you, and will send an answer? Are you and your prayers and intercessions a threat to the kingdom of darkness?*

**<u>Prayer is one surefire way for us to defeat the enemy!</u>** In order for us to do so, we have to know the right way to pray and develop effective prayer strategies. Prayer is a discipleship essential that every Believer needs to harness and master.

Join me and thousands of women from across the globe, as we study about Prayer! You're in for the journey of your life and I know after you finish this Bible Study, your life - your prayer life will never, ever be the same! Let's dig in and get started!

**Dance with the King!**

*Angelica*

## Lesson 1
# Introduction
## (Praying Scripture)

After this manner therefore pray ye:
Our Father which art in heaven, Hallowed be thy name.

Thy kingdom come, Thy will be done in earth, as it is in heaven.

Give us this day our daily bread.

And forgive us our debts, as we forgive our debtors.

And lead us not into temptation, but deliver us from evil:
For thine is the kingdom, and the power, and the glory, for ever.
Amen.

(Matthew 6:9-13)

# Pre-Work

## Read
Matthew 6:9-13

## Copywork
Write this week's verse 3x's each below. (Try writing in cursive for more of a challenge!) Check out the Journal Pages provided, at the end of this week's lesson for more space to write!

# Lesson Commentary

## Video Lesson

(You c watch this week's video lesson here: https://proverbs31businesswoman.com/prayer-bible-study-lesson-1)

P.S. I'd LOVE it if you left a comment on my blog and shared it with your friends on social media!

## Biblical Terminology

As you watch this week's video, we will study different words, from the passage of scripture, by looking them up in Strong's Concordance. Our purpose with this, is to gain a fuller, deeper understanding of the Hebrew meanings of the words. This is what helps us to have a better interpretation of scripture and its context. Some also call this method transliterating scripture to extract meaning. You can write the words and their meanings, in the space provided below:

# Prayer Strategy

This week, we are focusing on **PRAYING SCRIPTURE,** as our prayer strategy. Here are some practical ways you can apply this strategy:

• **Find scripture.** For every area or situation you are praying about, search the scriptures for a solution.

• **Read the scripture aloud.** This does two things – it speaks the Word of God into the atmosphere. God hears it and he respond to His Word being spoken. Remember God spoke the earth into existence. We should also speak the Word of God over situations in our lives. Secondly, we increase our faith when we hear the Word of God. It also does neat things to our brains and memory, when anything is read aloud. *"Faith comes by hearing and hearing by the Word of God. (Romans 10:17)*

• **Make it personal.** There are so many ways you can do this by inserting your name or the person's name, applying your situation – just be sure to keep with the context of scripture and not to deviate, in any way.

Always have your bible wide open, so you can pray the scriptures! When we do, we can have confidence that God not only hears our prayers, but he'll respond. When you pray the Word, you are praying the will of God!

> *Now this is the confidence that we have in Him, that if we ask anything according to His will, He hears us. And if we know that He hears us, whatever we ask, we know that we have the petitions that we have asked of Him.*
> *(I John 5:14-15)*

If you have more ways, be sure to share them, with me, on social media! (Facebook, Twitter, Instagram, Pinterest: @angelicakduncan)

***Spend this week, with your bible wide open, praying scripture. You can use the examples I've shared with you, in this week's lesson. Ask the Holy Spirit to show you how to make theses scripture-prayers more personal to you and your life. Remember, praying the Word of God is a surefire way for God to not only hear your prayers, but for the enemy to retreat.***

Feel free to use the Journal Pages, to write down any revelation or insights you receive from the Holy Spirit. This is also a great place to write down areas where you would like to pray, for guidance, wisdom, and correction. Anything the Holy Spirit brings to you,write it down! Then get to praying!

# Notes & Journaling

# Notes & Journaling

# Notes & Journaling

_____

_____

_____

_____

_____

_____

_____

_____

_____

_____

_____

_____

_____

_____

_____

# Notes & Journaling

_____

_____

_____

_____

_____

_____

_____

_____

_____

_____

_____

_____

_____

_____

_____

# Reflections & Questions

Over the next week, take some time to reflect and answer the following discussion questions.

1. What is prayer?

2. What is the purpose of prayer?

3. What are the types of prayers described in the Bible?

4. What are some of the prayer positions described in the Bible?

5. How much of your time is dedicated to prayer, talking to God, and seeking His will? How can you be purposeful about spending more time in prayer?

6. Do you find praying to God comfortable or a bit scary? Why is this?

7. What are your thoughts about the Lord's Prayer being more than just a recitation of a passage of scripture, but more so, a model for prayer? Does this confirm anything for you? Does it shed new light?

8. How have you seen effective prayer, like we discussed in James 5:16 or 2 Chronicles 7:14, used to change the outcome of situations? Describe the situation and key points, you believe, made this prayer effective and heard by God. (This can be something you've personally experienced or witnessed from afar.)

## Lesson 2
# Hallowed Be Thy Name
## (Praise & Worship)

*After this manner therefore pray ye:*
*Our Father which art in heaven, Hallowed be thy name.*

(Matthew 6:9)

# Pre-Work

## Read
Matthew 6:9

## Copywork
Write this week's verse 3x's each below. (Try writing in cursive for more of a challenge!) Check out the journal pages provided, at the end of this week's lesson for more space to write!

# Lesson Commentary

## Video Lesson

(You can watch this week's video lesson here: https://proverbs31businesswoman.com/prayer-bible-study-lesson-2)

P.S. I'd LOVE it if you left a comment on my blog and shared it with your friends on social media!

## Biblical Terminology

As you watch this week's video, we will study different words, from the passage of scripture, by looking them up in Strong's Concordance. Our purpose with this, is to gain a fuller, deeper understanding of the Hebrew meanings of the words. This is what helps us to have a better interpretation of scripture and its context. Some also call this method transliterating scripture to extract meaning. You can write the words and their meanings, in the space provided below:

# Prayer Strategy

This week, we are focusing on **PRAISE & WORSHIP,** as our prayer strategy. Here are some practical ways you can apply this strategy:

• Exalt the name of God
• Praise God for being holy
• Recognize God for who he is to you
• Praise him for being your heavenly Father (Abba)
• Praise God for being His other characteristics or names
• Play music that praises God's name, evokes you to praise Him, and invites His presence, with you.

*But the hour is coming, and now is, when the true worshipers will worship the Father in spirit and truth; for the Father is seeking such to worship Him.*
*(John 4:23)*

If you have more ways, be sure to share them, with me, on social media! (Facebook, Twitter, Instagram, Pinterest: @angelicakduncan)

***This week, in prayer, spend your time getting comfortable with God. Greet him, as you would a close family member or friend. Yes, He is holy, but he also longs to communicate with you, intimately and authentically. Talk to him all day long. He'll draw nigh to you, as you draw nigh to Him!***

Feel free to use the Journal Pages to write down any revelation or insights you receive from the Holy Spirit. This is also a great place to write down areas where you would like to pray, for guidance, wisdom, and correction. Anything the Holy Spirit brings to you, write it down! Then get to praying!

# Notes & Journaling

# Notes & Journaling

# Notes & Journaling

# Notes & Journaling

# Reflections & Questions

Over the next week, take some time to reflect and answer the following discussion questions.

**1. Who is God to you? Find one scripture to support your stance, on this belief.**

**2. How do you relate to God as "Father"? What emotions are evoked when you consider this? Does how you see God as Father have a correlation, with your relationship, with your earthly father?**

**3. List all of the names of God you know and describe how God has manifested himself to you, in those ways.**

**4. What is praise? What is the purpose of praise? Does this differ from what you believed or were taught?**

**5. What is worship? What is the purpose of worship? Does this differ from what you believed or were taught?**

**6. Think of some practical and purposeful ways you can praise, reverence, and honor God, in your daily life. List them below.**

**7. What are your thoughts about the praise being more than the "fast" songs and worship being more than the "slow" songs, at church or you hear on the radio? Does this confirm anything for you? Does it shed new light?**

**8. When considering this part of the Lord's prayer, as a greeting and salutation, write a few personal, heartfelt greetings you can make to God, as you go to him in prayer.**

# Lesson 3
# Thy Kingdom Come
## (God's Agenda)

Thy kingdom come, Thy will be done in earth, as it is in heaven.

(Matthew 6:10)

# Pre-Work

## Read
Matthew 6:10

## Copywork
Write this week's verse 3x's each below. (Try writing in cursive for more of a challenge!) Check out the journal pages provided, at the end of this week's lesson for more space to write!

# Lesson Commentary

## Video Lesson

(You can watch this week's video lesson here: https://proverbs31businesswoman.com/prayer-bible-study-lesson-3)

P.S. I'd LOVE it if you left a comment on my blog and shared it with your friends on social media!

## Biblical Terminology

As you watch this week's video, we will study different words, from the passage of scripture, by looking them up in Strong's Concordance. Our purpose with this, is to gain a fuller, deeper understanding of the Hebrew meanings of the words. This is what helps us to have a better interpretation of scripture and its context. Some also call this method transliterating scripture to extract meaning. You can write the words and their meanings, in the space provided below:

# Prayer Strategy

This week, we are focusing on **GOD'S AGENDA,** as our prayer strategy. Here are some practical ways you can apply this strategy:

• Pray the will of God to unfold in the pressing areas of your life and the lives of those who have made prayer requests to you (marriage, children, household, finances, health, giving, opportunities, etc.)
• Pray for your husband, children, family, friends to follow God's agenda for their lives.
• Pray for salvation and deliverance for those in your family circle.
• Pray for your supervisors and the many decision makers (CEO, HR, Accounting, etc.) where you and/or your husband works – that they operate with Godly principles. (Something extra I do…pray for salvation in their lives, peace in their homes, and financial security.)
• Pray for God's will to permeate the schools in your local community. Especially pray for the Christian educators, staff, and children that they are used as light and salt in the school system.
• Pray for those in government positions (President, King, Prime minister, Governor, Mayor, Senate, Councilmen, Judges, District Attorneys, etc.) to be sensitive to the will of God and the Holy Spirit and create/defend laws and policies that are Godly and fair to all citizens.
• Pray for all those, in the Body of Christ, to remain faithful to the agenda and mission of God of spreading the Gospel and making disciples
• Pray for the return of Jesus Christ

*I can of Myself do nothing. As I hear, I judge; and My judgment is righteous, because I do not seek My own will but the will of the Father who sent Me.*
*(John 5:30)*

If you have more ways, be sure to share them, with me, on social media! (Facebook, Twitter, Instagram, Pinterest: @angelicakduncan)

***During prayer this week, spend time seeking and listening to the will of God. It doesn't matter what situation you're praying about (family, friends, yourself, healing, wisdom, etc.) Ask the Holy Spirit to reveal the will of God to you. This way you'll be empowered with the truth and can pray effectively!***

Feel free to use the Journal Pages to write down any revelation or insights you receive from the Holy Spirit. This is also a great place to write down areas where you would like to pray, for guidance, wisdom, and correction. Anything the Holy Spirit brings to you, write it down! Then get to praying!

# Notes & Journaling

# Notes & Journaling

_____

_____

_____

_____

_____

_____

_____

_____

_____

_____

_____

_____

_____

_____

_____

_____

# Notes & Journaling

# Notes & Journaling

# Reflections & Questions

Over the next week, take some time to reflect and answer the following discussion questions.

1. What is the Kingdom of God?

2. What is God's will for all of mankind?

3. How can you get to know the will of God, the Father, for your life?

4. What is the meaning of "in earth, as it is in heaven"?

5. Where do you see God's Kingdom "come," in your life? Your community? Your city? Your State? Your Country?

6. How can you pray for God's Kingdom to come, in the earth? Be specific.

7. Have you ever had a time where you thought you were praying God's will and did not get results - only to discover you were wrong about God's will for that situation. If so, describe it. How did this impact the way you began to seek God and pray differently?

8. Consider how praying God's Kingdom come and His Will being done, in earth, impacts the way you pray. What does this mean to you? Are there any adjustments you'll begin making, in your prayer life, as a result of this?

## Lesson 4

# Our Daily Bread
## (The Lord's Provision)

Give us this day our daily bread.

(Matthew 6:11)

# Pre-Work

## Read
Matthew 6:11

## Copywork
Write this week's verse 3x's each below. (Try writing in cursive for more of a challenge!) Check out the journal pages provided, at the end of this week's lesson for more space to write!

# Lesson Commentary

## Video Lesson

(You can watch this week's video lesson here: https://proverbs31businesswoman.com/prayer-bible-study-lesson-4)

P.S. I'd LOVE it if you left a comment on my blog and shared it with your friends on social media!

## Biblical Terminology

As you watch this week's video, we will study different words, from the passage of scripture, by looking them up in Strong's Concordance. Our purpose with this, is to gain a fuller, deeper understanding of the Hebrew meanings of the words. This is what helps us to have a better interpretation of scripture and its context. Some also call this method transliterating scripture to extract meaning. You can write the words and their meanings, in the space provided below:

# Prayer Strategy

This week, we are focusing on **THE LORD'S PROVISION,** as our prayer strategy. Here are some practical ways you can apply this strategy:

• Acknowledge God, as Jehovah Jireh – The Lord, My Provider
• Ask God to meet your daily needs, providing for you and your family (food, clothing, shelter, transportation, finances, etc.)
• Ask God for spiritual "manna" through His Word to encourage you, confirm His truths and promises, and correct/redirect you towards His will for your life.
• Pray for God to be the "Daily Bread" for others in your circle and community.
• Ask God to open your eyes and heart to see the need of others and to be moved to help meet those needs.

*And Abraham called the name of the place, The-Lord-Will-Provide (Jehovahjireh); as it is said to this day, "In the Mount of the Lord it shall be provided."*
*(Genesis 22:14)*

If you have more ways, be sure to share them, with me, on social media! (Facebook, Twitter, Instagram, Pinterest: @angelicakduncan)

***This week, as you pray, surrender your own ideas about your personal needs, to God. Begin trusting Him, in a new way, to not only meet your needs, but to exceed your expectations! Also take a moment to consider the needs of others. Pray and ask God to show you how you can be the hands and feet of Jesus to meet those needs.***

Feel free to use the Journal Pages to write down any revelation or insights you receive from the Holy Spirit. This is also a great place to write down areas where you would like to pray, for guidance, wisdom, and correction. Anything the Holy Spirit brings to you, write it down! Then get to praying!

# Notes & Journaling

# Notes & Journaling

# Notes & Journaling

_____

_____

_____

_____

_____

_____

_____

_____

_____

_____

_____

_____

_____

_____

_____

_____

_____

_____

# Notes & Journaling

# Reflections & Questions

Over the next week, take some time to reflect and answer the following discussion questions.

1. What is the meaning of "our daily bread"?

2. What are your daily needs and provisions? Do you really trust God to meet those, for you?

3. Think of a time, when you had an urgent need, describe how God met that need and provided for you, through prayer, faith, and using people and/or community.

4. What is the interpretation of Jevhoah-Jireh? Does this shift your understanding about this aspect of God's character?

5. List some ways you can relate, "give us this day our daily bread," to God being Jehovah Jireh (The Lord, my Provider), in your life.

6. How can you pray for the needs of others, in your community to be met?

7. Even though we live in a very independent, self-reliant, self-focused society, how can you shift this worldview, in your life and the life of your family? What can you do to be more dependent on God, for even the smallest, seemingly insignificant, of your needs? (Think about the Israelites depending upon God daily for Manna from Heaven.)

8. How can you be less selfish with your time and resources and be more like the hands and feet of Jesus, by availing yourself to God, to meet the needs of others? List some practical ways you can do this.

## Lesson 5

# Forgive Us, As We Forgive
## (The Power of Forgiveness)

*And forgive us our debts, as we forgive our debtors.*

(Matthew 6:12)

# Pre-Work

## Read
Matthew 6:12

## Copywork
Write this week's verse 3x's each below. (Try writing in cursive for more of a challenge!) Check out the journal pages provided, at the end of this week's lesson for more space to write!

# Lesson Commentary

## Video Lesson

(You can watch this week's video lesson here: https://proverbs31businesswoman.com/prayer-bible-study-lesson-5)

P.S. I'd LOVE it if you left a comment on my blog and shared it with your friends on social media!

## Biblical Terminology

As you watch this week's video, we will study different words, from the passage of scripture, by looking them up in Strong's Concordance. Our purpose with this, is to gain a fuller, deeper understanding of the Hebrew meanings of the words. This is what helps us to have a better interpretation of scripture and its context. Some also call this method transliterating scripture to extract meaning. You can write the words and their meanings, in the space provided below:

# Prayer Strategy

This week, we are focusing on **THE POWER OF FORGIVENESS,** as our prayer strategy. Here are some practical ways you can apply this strategy:

• Recognize that forgiveness of sins is because of the blood of Jesus that what shed on the cross and his Resurrection 3 days later. It is through Jesus we have forgiveness from God and should forgive others.
• Consider the areas of your life where you've fallen short and missed the mark – ask God for forgiveness, repent and commit to moving forward, in a renewed way.
• Ask the Holy Spirit to search your heart for unforgiveness and hidden bitterness towards another person – release that, forgive them, ask God to forgive you. Pray for them and truly forgive, even if they never acknowledge the wrong they've done.
• Seek those people whom you need to ask forgiveness. Lean on the Holy Spirit on how to approach the situation. If the person is no longer available, then ask God for forgiveness and release yourself from the weight of that sin. ***Don't walk in condemnation.***
• Pray for those who have made themselves enemies of you, your circle, your community…but mostly God. Ask the Holy Spirit to move in their heart towards Jesus.

Always have your bible wide open, so you can pray the scriptures! When we do, we can have confidence that God not only hears our prayers, but he'll respond. When you pray the Word, you are praying the will of God!

> *If we confess our sins, He is faithful and just to forgive us our sins and to cleanse us from all unrighteousness.*
> *(1 John 1:9)*

If you have more ways, be sure to share them, with me, on social media! (Facebook, Twitter, Instagram, Pinterest: @angelicakduncan)

***Spend this week in prayer, asking the Holy Spirit to examine your heart regarding unforgiveness, bitterness, and resentment towards others. As He reveals these dark areas, in your heart, write them down, and commit to truly walking in forgiveness. Remember forgiveness is not letting someone off the hook, for their wrongdoing. Forgiveness is about no longer having the need to demand or require payment for an offense. It's putting Justice in the hands of God, the Father.***

Feel free to use the Journal Pages to write down any revelation or insights you receive from the Holy Spirit. This is also a great place to write down areas where you would like to pray, for guidance, wisdom, and correction. Anything the Holy Spirit brings to you, write it down! Then get to praying!

# Notes & Journaling

# Notes & Journaling

---

---

---

---

---

---

---

---

---

---

---

---

---

---

---

---

---

---

---

---

# Notes & Journaling

# Notes & Journaling

---
---
---
---
---
---
---
---
---
---
---
---
---
---
---
---
---

# Reflections & Questions

Over the next week, take some time to reflect and answer the following discussion questions.

1. **What does it mean to be in debt? How are we in debt (or debtors) to God?**


2. **What does it mean to forgive?**


3. **Why do we need to ask for forgiveness from God? From others?**


4. **What is the significance of "forgive us, as we forgive"?**


5. **Think of a time, when you sinned against another person, how quickly were you to ask for forgiveness? Did that person continue to hold your mistake over your head or did they truly forgive and move on?**


6. **Think about when some sinned against you. How quickly did you forgive them? Did you wait for an apology before you forgave? Did you forgive but not forget?**


7. **Who do you need to truly forgive? How did they sin against you?**


8. **What steps do you need to take to "instantaneously forgive" others? How will this make you more like Christ?**

## Lesson 6
# Deliver Us From Evil
## (Divine Protection & Help)

*And lead us not into temptation, but deliver us from evil:*

*(Matthew 6:13a)*

# Pre-Work

## Read
Matthew 6:13a

## Copywork
Write this week's verse 3x's each below. (Try writing in cursive for more of a challenge!) Check out the journal pages provided, at the end of this week's lesson for more space to write!

# Lesson Commentary

## Video Lesson

(You can watch this week's video lesson here: https://proverbs31businesswoman.com/prayer-bible-study-lesson-6)

P.S. I'd LOVE it if you left a comment on my blog and shared it with your friends on social media!

## Biblical Terminology

As you watch this week's video, we will study different words, from the passage of scripture, by looking them up in Strong's Concordance. Our purpose with this, is to gain a fuller, deeper understanding of the Hebrew meanings of the words. This is what helps us to have a better interpretation of scripture and its context. Some also call this method transliterating scripture to extract meaning. You can write the words and their meanings, in the space provided below:

# Prayer Strategy

This week, we are focusing on **DIVINE PROTECTION & HELP,** as our prayer strategy. Here are some practical ways you can apply this strategy:

• Acknowledge God's Sovereignty in your life and any trials or challenges you may be facing. There's nothing happening that He's not aware of – you are not alone and God is still on the throne!
• Ask God to help you and others navigate your trials and challenges, in such a way, it brings Him Glory and provides an avenue for growth.
• Pray for assurance of salvation to be made known, during trials.
• Ask God to protect you and others from all things evil – people, places, things, ideas, thoughts, spiritual wickedness, political powers, attitudes, mindsets, etc.
• Pray for Christians who are experiencing persecution and torture around the world, for the sake of Christ, to be comforted by the Holy Spirit and they stand strong in their faith.
• Pray for areas of heightened activity or "hot spots" (wars, conflicts, political uprisings, terrorism, earthquakes, floods, tornadoes, hurricanes, tsunamis, an other natural or man-made disasters).

Always have your bible wide open, so you can pray the scriptures! When we do, we can have confidence that God not only hears our prayers, but he'll respond. When you pray the Word, you are praying the will of God!

*And He said to me, "My grace is sufficient for you, for My strength is made perfect in weakness." Therefore most gladly I will rather boast in my infirmities, that the power of Christ may rest upon me.*
*(2 Corinthians 12:9)*

If you have more ways, be sure to share them, with me, on social media! (Facebook, Twitter, Instagram, Pinterest: @angelicakduncan)

***During your prayer time this week, be intentional about confessing your areas of weakness to God. Then, ask him to help you submit to Him, resist the devil, so he will flee. Also, invite God to reveal His Glory and purpose, to you, as you journey through your trials and challenges you may be facing. Remember, even in difficulties and weaknesses, God's power is made perfect, in our weakness!***

Feel free to use the Journal Pages to write down any revelation or insights you receive from the Holy Spirit. This is also a great place to write down areas where you would like to pray, for guidance, wisdom, and correction. Anything the Holy Spirit brings to you, write it down! Then get to praying!

# Notes & Journaling

# Notes & Journaling

# Notes & Journaling

# Notes & Journaling

_____

_____

_____

_____

_____

_____

_____

_____

_____

_____

_____

_____

_____

_____

_____

_____

_____

_____

# Reflections & Questions

Over the next week, take some time to reflect and answer the following discussion questions.

1. What is a temptation, according to this passage of scripture?

2. What are some of the misconceptions about the meaning of this passage of scripture? Have you been guilty of believing this? How has your understanding grown?

3. Have you ever considered asking God to help you to not sin, when you are tempted to do so, anyways? Why or why not?

4. Think of a time when you were faced with the temptation of sinning, but you chose, instead, not to sin, describe how you were able to navigate this choice and not sin against God. Do you now see that, as a way to glorify God?

5. Why do you believe, as Christians, we often want to avoid trials? How can God ordained trials be useful to our growth and maturity, as Christians?

6. Do you see temptation as an opportunity to glorify God? What about abstaining from the appearance of evil, as a way to show your love for the Lord?

7. We know that every trial is not necessarily of God. Some trials we face because of bad decisions we've made. Despite this, how have situations, like these, still worked out for your good, anyways? How have you seen God's handiwork, even in your bad decision making?

8. Describe other ways you can glorify God or allow His Glory to be revealed in the earth.

# Lesson 7
# The Kingdom, Power, & Glory
## (The Doxology)

For thine is the kingdom, and the power, and the glory, for ever. Amen.

(Matthew 6:13b)

# Pre-Work

## Read
Matthew 6:13b

## Copywork
Write this week's verse 3x's each below. (Try writing in cursive for more of a challenge!) Check out the journal pages provided, at the end of this week's lesson for more space to write!

# Lesson Commentary

## Video Lesson

(You can watch this week's video lesson here: https://proverbs31businesswoman.com/prayer-bible-study-lesson-7)

P.S. I'd LOVE it if you left a comment on my blog and shared it with your friends on social media!

## Biblical Terminology

As you watch this week's video, we will study different words, from the passage of scripture, by looking them up in Strong's Concordance. Our purpose with this, is to gain a fuller, deeper understanding of the Hebrew meanings of the words. This is what helps us to have a better interpretation of scripture and its context. Some also call this method transliterating scripture to extract meaning. You can write the words and their meanings, in the space provided below:

# Prayer Strategy

This week, we are focusing on the **DOXOLGY**, as our prayer strategy. Here are some practical ways you can apply this strategy:

• Acknowledge God's Kingdom, Power, and Glory in all areas of your life, those in your circle, and in the earth
• Praise God for his Majesty and Splendor! Stand in awe of Him, who He is, and what He's created! Look for God in everything (nature, people, art, architecture, technology, literature, etc.)
• Thank God for his Agenda (Will) being done on earth and let him know you are believing and walking in faith concerning His promises.
• Affirm your belief and assurance that God hears your prayers with "Amen" - so it is, so be it, may it be fulfilled – your absolute trust and confidence that He's going to attend to the words of your prayers!

Always have your bible wide open, so you can pray the scriptures! When we do, we can have confidence that God not only hears our prayers, but he'll respond. When you pray the Word, you are praying the will of God!

*But seek first the kingdom of God and His righteousness, and all these things shall be added to you.*
*(Matthew 6:33)*

If you have more ways, be sure to share them, with me, on social media! (Facebook, Twitter, Instagram, Pinterest: @angelicakduncan)

*Spend this week in prayer, letting God know that you are availing yourself, to establishing his Kingdom, submitting to his Power, and manifesting His Glory, in the earth. Ask for revelation about what that looks like and how your purpose and vision are aligned to this. Also, ask the Holy Spirit to reveal any areas in your life, habits, friends, places, etc. that are not aligned with your purpose and could prohibit your progress, in this area. Big thing here is, to allow yourself to be in a position to receive instruction and insight into a deeper understanding of God's purpose and plans, for your life...then boldly walk in faith towards the goal!*

Feel free to use the Journal Pages to write down any revelation or insights you receive from the Holy Spirit. This is also a great place to write down areas where you would like to pray, for guidance, wisdom, and correction. Anything the Holy Spirit brings to you, write it down! Then get to praying!

# Notes & Journaling

_____

_____

_____

_____

_____

_____

_____

_____

_____

_____

_____

_____

_____

_____

_____

_____

# Notes & Journaling

# Notes & Journaling

_____

_____

_____

_____

_____

_____

_____

_____

_____

_____

_____

_____

_____

_____

_____

_____

# Notes & Journaling

---

---

---

---

---

---

---

---

---

---

---

---

---

---

---

---

---

---

---

---

# Reflections & Questions

Over the next week, take some time to reflect and answer the following discussion questions:

**1. How can you relate Psalm 103:19 "His kingdom rules over all" to the understanding of God's Kingdom?**

**2. What is "omnipotent control"? Describe how God is displaying that in the world today. Can you also see this, in your life?**

**3. Describe God's power in your own words.**

**4. What are the two meanings of the Word "glory"? How do these two meanings relate?**

**5. How is God's character related to His glory? How are YOU related to God's Glory? What's your role in revealing God's Glory in the earth?**

**6. "Forever" is actually two words "for" and "ever." How did studying these words and their meaning give you deeper understanding of who God is and his splendor, wonder, and power?**

**7. What is the universal meaning of "Amen." What insight have you gained from the study and understanding of this word?**

**8. How does this final verse, in the Lord's Prayer, help us to keep the right focus, heart-set, and perspective, in prayer?**

## Lesson 8

# Conclusion
## (Modeling Prayer)

After this manner therefore pray ye:
Our Father which art in heaven, Hallowed be thy name.

Thy kingdom come, Thy will be done in earth, as it is in heaven.

Give us this day our daily bread.

And forgive us our debts, as we forgive our debtors.

And lead us not into temptation, but deliver us from evil:
For thine is the kingdom, and the power, and the glory, for ever.
Amen.

(Matthew 6:9-13)

# Lesson Commentary

## Video Lesson

(You can watch this week's video lesson here: https://proverbs31businesswoman.com/
prayer-bible-study-lesson-8)

P.S. I'd LOVE it if you left a comment on my blog and shared it with your friends on
social media!

# Prayer Strategy

This week, we are going to use the Lord's Prayer, for the purpose of **MODELING PRAYER.** We've spent the last 6 weeks dissecting each component. This is where we put everything together! Here are some things you'll need, to make this time more effective, fulfilling, invigorating, and sweet, for you:

• **Your Bible.** As you pray you want to make sure you are including scripture into your prayers. God responds to His Word. Say it and pray it back to Him!

• **Your journal and pen.** (I've provided journal pages for you already.) You'll need this to write down anything that comes to your mind, as your praying. Sometimes, God will begin answering our prayers to us, as we pray. Other times, the Holy Spirit may reveal other things to you about a certain situation. Both will help you pray more effectively.

• **Praise and worship music.** This can be an effective tool, if you choose the right music – music that is truly praise and worship. This will help usher in the presence of God and set an atmosphere that's sweet to just hang out with God.

• **Dedicated and quiet place.** You can have your home office, a corner in your room, your bedside, even a closet, your laundry room, or your kitchen floor. It doesn't matter! You just want to have a spot that's quiet and away from distractions. Try to make it the same place, if possible.

• **Set an appointment with God & Yourself.** Pick a time of day you will dedicate to praying. It can be in the morning before you get your day started. Midday, during your lunch, or in the evenings with your family, before bed. Two big things here: Be consistent. Don't be condemned. Life happens and God's not holding your prayer time over your head. This should be something special that you can't wait to get to! If something happens and you can't, no worries! Pray where you are. God will meet you there!

• **Water and light snack.** This will keep you refreshed and alert, as you're praying, especially if you pray for a long time.

Always have your bible wide open, so you can pray the scriptures! When we do, we can have confidence that God not only hears our prayers, but he'll respond. When you pray the Word, you are praying the will of God!

*"Come now, and let us reason together," Says the LORD.*
*(Isaiah 1:18)*

*Now this is the confidence that we have in Him, that if we ask anything according to His will, He hears us. And if we know that He hears us, whatever we ask, we know that we have the petitions that we have asked of Him.*
*(I John 5:14-15)*

**Let's get to praying!**

# Hallowed Be Thy Name
## (Praise & Worship)

*After this manner therefore pray ye:*
*Our Father which art in heaven, Hallowed be thy name.*

(Matthew 6:9)

We are focusing on **PRAISE,** as our prayer strategy. Here are some practical ways you can apply this strategy:

• Exalt the name of God
• Praise God for being holy
• Recognize God for who he is to you
• Praise him for being your heavenly Father (Abba)
• Praise God for being His other characteristics or names
• Play music that praises God's name, evokes you to praise Him, and invites His presence, with you.

*But the hour is coming, and now is, when the true worshipers will worship the Father in spirit and truth;*
*for the Father is seeking such to worship Him.*
*(John 4:23)*

# Notes & Journaling

_____

_____

_____

_____

_____

_____

_____

_____

_____

_____

_____

_____

_____

_____

_____

_____

# Thy Kingdom Come
## (God's Agenda)

*Thy kingdom come, Thy will be done in earth, as it is in heaven.*

*(Matthew 6:10)*

For this component, we are focusing on **GOD'S AGENDA,** as our prayer strategy. Here are some practical ways you can apply this strategy:

• Pray the will of God to unfold in the pressing areas of your life and the lives of those who have made prayer requests to you (marriage, children, household, finances, health, giving, opportunities, etc.)
• Pray for your husband, children, family, friends to follow God's agenda for their lives.
• Pray for salvation and deliverance for those in your family circle.
• Pray for your supervisors and the many decision makers (CEO, HR, Accounting, etc.) where you and/or your husband works – that they operate with Godly principles. (Something extra I do…pray for salvation in their lives, peace in their homes, and financial security.)
• Pray for God's will to permeate the schools in your local community. Especially pray for the Christian educators, staff, and children that they are used as light and salt in the school system.
• Pray for those in government positions (President, King, Prime minister, Governor, Mayor, Senate, Councilmen, Judges, District Attorneys, etc.) to be sensitive to the will of God and the Holy Spirit and create/defend laws and policies that are Godly and fair to all citizens.
• Pray for all those, in the Body of Christ, to remain faithful to the agenda and mission of God of spreading the Gospel and making disciples
• Pray for the return of Jesus Christ

*I can of Myself do nothing. As I hear, I judge; and My judgment is righteous, because I do not seek My own will but the will of the Father who sent Me.*
*(John 5:30)*t

# Notes & Journaling

_____

_____

_____

_____

_____

_____

_____

_____

_____

_____

_____

_____

_____

_____

_____

_____

_____

# Our Daily Bread
## (The Lord's Provision)

*Give us this day our daily bread.*

*(Matthew 6:11)*

For this component, we are focusing on **THE LORD'S PROVISION,** as our prayer strategy. Here are some practical ways you can apply this strategy:

• Acknowledge God, as Jehovah Jireh – The Lord, My Provider
• Ask God to meet your daily needs, providing for you and your family (food, clothing, shelter, transportation, finances, etc.)
• Ask God for spiritual "manna" through His Word to encourage you, confirm His truths and promises, and correct/redirect you towards His will for your life.
• Pray for God to be the "Daily Bread" for others in your circle and community.
• Ask God to open your eyes and heart to see the need of others and to be moved to help meet those needs.

*And Abraham called the name of the place, The-Lord-Will-Provide (Jehovahjireh); as it is said to this day, "In the Mount of the Lord it shall be provided."*
*(Genesis 22:14)*

# Notes & Journaling

# Forgive Us, As We Forgive
## (The Power of Forgiveness)

*And forgive us our debts, as we forgive our debtors.*

(Matthew 6:12)

For this component, we are focusing on **FORGIVENESS,** as our prayer strategy. Here are some practical ways you can apply this strategy:

• Recognize that forgiveness of sins is because of the blood of Jesus that what shed on the cross and his Resurrection 3 days later. It is through Jesus we have forgiveness from God and should forgive others.
• Consider the areas of your life where you've fallen short and missed the mark – ask God for forgiveness, repent and commit to moving forward, in a renewed way.
• Ask the Holy Spirit to search your heart for unforgiveness and hidden bitterness towards another person – release that, forgive them, ask God to forgive you. Pray for them and truly forgive, even if they never acknowledge the wrong they've done.
• Seek those people whom you need to ask forgiveness. Lean on the Holy Spirit on how to approach the situation. If the person is no longer available, then ask God forgiveness and release yourself from the weight of that sin. Don't walk in condemnation.
• Pray for those who have made themselves enemies of you, your circle…but mostly God. Ask the Holy Spirit to move in their heart towards Jesus.

Always have your bible wide open, so you can pray the scriptures! When we do, we can have confidence that God not only hears our prayers, but he'll respond. When you pray the Word, you are praying the will of God!

*If we confess our sins, He is faithful and just to forgive us our sins and to cleanse us from all unrighteousness.*
*(1 John 1:9)*

# Notes & Journaling

# Deliver Us From Evil
## (Divine Protection & Help)

*And lead us not into temptation, but deliver us from evil:*

(Matthew 6:13a)

For this component, we are focusing on **DIVINE PROTECTION & HELP,** as our prayer strategy. Here are some practical ways you can apply this strategy:

• Acknowledge God's Sovereignty in your life and any trials or challenges you may be facing. There's nothing happening that He's not aware of – you are not alone and God is still on the throne!
• Ask God to help you and others navigate your trials and challenges, in such a way, it brings Him Glory and provides an avenue for growth.
• Pray for assurance of salvation to be made known, during trials.
• Ask God to protect you and others from all things evil – people, places, things, ideas, thoughts, spiritual wickedness, political powers, attitudes, mindsets, etc.
• Pray for Christians who are experiencing persecution and torture around the world, for the sake of Christ, to be comforted by the Holy Spirit and they stand strong in their faith.
• Pray for areas of heightened activity or "hot spots" (wars, conflicts, political uprisings, terrorism, earthquakes, floods, tornadoes, hurricanes, tsunamis, an other natural or man-made disasters).

Always have your bible wide open, so you can pray the scriptures! When we do, we can have confidence that God not only hears our prayers, but he'll respond. When you pray the Word, you are praying the will of God!

*And He said to me, "My grace is sufficient for you, for My strength is made perfect in weakness." Therefore most gladly I will rather boast in my infirmities, that the power of Christ may rest upon me.*
*(2 Corinthians 12:9)*

# Notes & Journaling

# The Kingdom, Power, & Glory
## (The Doxology)

*For thine is the kingdom, and the power, and the glory, for ever.
Amen.*

*(Matthew 6:13b)*

For this component, we are focusing on the **DOXOLGY**, as our prayer strategy. Here are some practical ways you can apply this strategy:

• Acknowledge God's Kingdom, Power, and Glory in all areas of your life, those in your circle, and in the earth
• Praise God for his Majesty and Splendor! Stand in awe of Him, who He is, and what He's created! Look for God in everything (nature, people, art, architecture, technology, literature, etc.)
• Thank God for his Agenda (Will) being done on earth and let him know you are believing and walking in faith concerning His promises.
• Affirm your belief and assurance that God hears your prayers with "Amen" - so it is, so be it, may it be fulfilled – your absolute trust and confidence that He's going to attend to the words of your prayers!

*But seek first the kingdom of God and His righteousness, and all these things shall be added to you.*
*(Matthew 6:33)*

# Notes & Journaling

# Reflections & Questions

Over the next week, take some time to reflect and answer the following discussion questions:

**1. Now that you've prayed through the Lord's Prayer, how has your perspective changed about reciting vs. praying this prayer fervently?**

**2. Over the last 8 weeks, how have you grown in your prayer life?**

**3. In what ways has your understanding about prayer grown?**

**4. How will you approach prayer moving forward?**

**5. How has God opened up your eyes about your role with prayer (and possibly intercession), in the Body of Christ?**

**6. Were there any prayers answered, during this bible study, that previously you didn't seem to gain any ground, previously? I'd love for you to share them with me, on social media!**
**(Facebook, Twitter, Instagram, Pinterest: @angelicakduncan)**

**7. Are there any new prayer strategies you will begin implementing into your prayer time? Which ones and how do you plan to implement them?**

**8. Name 3-5 people you will share this bible study with and teach them about the importance, power, and strategy of prayer. Now, go make disciples! :)**

# Notes & Journaling

# Thank You for joining us!

**You just finished an amazing journey of studying your bible, learning about how to pray effectively & growing as a Disciple of Christ!**

I'd love your feedback on your experience with our Proverbs 31 Business Woman Community, this Bible Study & Companion Workbook, the video series, and any of the support materials and resources we provided you.

Your feedback is invaluable to me. It helps my team and I, to be able to, better design Bible Studies and provide resources for you to grow, in your walk with Christ as a woman, wife, mother, friend, and leader.

*You can give us your feedback, for this Bible Study here:*
https://proverbs31businesswoman.com/prayer-bible-study-feedback

Be sure to connect with Angelica on all of her social media pages. She is committed to making disciples and equipping you along the way! Join us!

Facebook
Twitter
Instagram
Pinterest
Snapchat

@angelicakduncan

**It's an honor to serve you!**

**Dance with the King!**

*Angelica*

Made in United States
Troutdale, OR
07/02/2023